About the Author

Pauline Rowson lives in the UK. She is the author of several marketing and self-help books and for many years ran her own successful marketing, PR and training company. She is an accomplished public speaker and is also the author of the popular marine mystery series of crime and thriller novels.

Books by Pauline Rowson

Crime Fiction – Marine Mysteries
DI Andy Horton novels
Tide of Death
Deadly Waters

In Cold Daylight
In for the Kill

Non-fiction
Marketing
Successful Selling
Telemarketing, Cold Calling & Appointment Making
Building a Positive Media Profile
Being Positive and Staying Positive
Communicating with more Confidence
Fundraising for your School
Publishing and Promoting your book

Praise for The Easy Step by Step Guides

MARKETING TO WIN MORE BUSINESS

The Easy Step by Step Guide

BY

PAULINE ROWSON

ROWMARK

First Published by Rowmark Limited in 2007
65 Rogers Mead
Hayling Island
Hampshire
England
PO11 0PL

First printed 2007
Copyright © Pauline Rowson 2007

ISBN 978 0 9548045 8 9

Other Easy Step by Step Guides

Sales and Marketing Books

Marketing
Successful Selling
Building a Positive Media Profile
Writing Advertising Copy
Writing Articles and Newsletters
Are Your Customers Being Served?
Telemarketing, Cold Calling & Appointment Making

Personal Development Books

Stress and Time Management
Communicating with more Confidence
Giving Confident Presentations
Being Positive and Staying Positive (even when the going gets tough)

Management Books

Motivating your Staff
Recruiting the Right Staff
Better Budgeting for your Business
Managing Change
Handling Confrontation
Writing a Business Plan and Making it Work
Negotiating for Success

Other books in the series

Publishing and Promoting your Book
Fundraising for your School

All the above guides are available from bookshops and online, and as eBooks.

Rowmark Limited
E-mail: enquiries@rowmark.co.uk
www.rowmark.co.uk

'I particularly like the boxes containing key statements and the easy to read and digest summaries – ideal for the busy person.'

'Clear, reader friendly and full of helpful hints.'

'I refer to my copy often and have found the summary sections and the highlighted hints invaluable.'

'A most practical, helpful guide.'

Easy Step by Step Guides

○   Quick and easy to read – from cover to cover in two hours

○   Contain a handy bullet point summary at the end of each chapter

○   Provide lots of tips and techniques

○   Have a simple style and layout – making the books easy to read

○   Jargon free – straightforward and easy to understand

○   Written by practitioners – people with experience and who are 'experts' in their subject.

Contents

Introduction..**13**
How to use this guide...13
What you will learn from this guide............................14

Chapter 1
Know your customers..**15**
Seven key marketing questions....................................15
What are the marketing tools?.....................................17
Choosing the right marketing tools............................20
In summary..25

Chapter 2
Know what your customers are buying............**26**
Benefits and features..26
Why people buy..28
Promoting a service...30
In summary..32

Chapter 3
The market place and marketing planning..........**33**
SWOT analysis..33
The marketing action plan..36
Set your marketing objectives.....................................37
Marketing strategies...39
In summary..41

Chapter 4
Advertising...**42**
Advertising Objectives...43
Advertising media...45
    Printed media...45
    Broadcast media..47
    Poster advertising..47
    Internet advertising...48
    'Off the Page' advertising.....................................49
    Direct response advertising..................................49
    Mailshot letters, leaflets, inserts into
    magazines and flyers, doordrop leaflets............50
    Signage...50
    E shots..51
    Promotional items...51
In summary...52

Chapter 5
How to make advertising and mailshots work....**53**
Advertising regulations..54
Making your advertising message work.......................55
    Attention..55
    Interest...58
    Desire...59
    Action...60
More about mailshots...61
In summary...63

Chapter 6
E-mail marketing...**65**
What you can and can't do –
business to consumer marketing...................................65
Buying in or renting a list from a third party...................67
What you can and can't do -
business to business marketing....................................69
Is it worth it? – Does e-mail marketing work?...............70
Benefits of an e-mail campaign...................................71
How to make your e-mail marketing more effective....72
Writing e-mail copy...72
Viral marketing..74
In summary..76

Chapter 7
Newsletters and eNewsletters.................**78**
Building a subscription list...79
Content is critical...80
Consistency and timing...80
Customer feedback...81
In summary..82

Chapter 8
Corporate brochures and web sites.........**84**
Corporate brochures...84
Web sites...86
What kind of structure do you need?...........................87
Content...87
In summary..90

Chapter 9
Exhibitions...**92**
Questions to ask before exhibiting..........................92
Before the exhibition...93
After the exhibition...95
In summary..96

Chapter 10
Sponsorship and sales promotion.........................**97**
Sponsorship...97
Sales promotion..99
Types of sales promotions.....................................100
In summary...103

Chapter 11
Building a media profile.....................................**105**
So what are your possible news stories?...................107
A word about angles...109
Where can you send your story?.............................110
Writing the news story..112
Writing your news release......................................114
Embargoes..115
Photo stories...115
Rules for good media relations...............................118
In summary...122

Chapter 12
Word of mouth...**123**
In summary...126

Introduction

Every organisation needs customers. In order to grow and survive you need to actively market your business, its services and products. And even if you are operating in the public sector, or in a non-profit organisation, there is still a need to communicate successfully with your target market.

This guide shows you how to use a variety of marketing techniques both traditional and Internet based to win more business.

How to use this guide

This guide is written in as clear a style as possible to aid you. I recommend that you read it through from beginning to end and then dip into it to refresh your memory. The boxes in each chapter contain tips to help you and at the end of each chapter is a useful summary of the points covered.

Note: To avoid confusion and the cumbersome use of 'he' and 'she', he has been adopted throughout this guide. No prejudice is intended.

What you will learn from this guide

This guide will show you:

○ how to target your customers and prospective customers

○ how to use the various promotional tools more successfully

○ how to make your advertising and direct mail more effective

○ how to integrate e-mail marketing and the Internet into your marketing strategy

○ how to conduct e mail campaigns, write e shots and e newsletters

○ how to win business at exhibitions

○ how to build media profile and write a news release

○ how to set up and exploit sponsorship opportunities.

Chapter 1

Know your customers

The key to successful marketing is in knowing your customers, understanding their needs and desires and communicating with them in an effective manner. Without this knowledge the marketing you undertake could be suspect and therefore a waste of time, money and energy. So, how well do you know your markets? Try answering the seven key questions below.

Seven key marketing questions

1.   **What business are you in?**

This is not as straightforward as it seems. For example if you are a book publisher then you might think that your business is printing and selling books but it isn't. Depending upon the types of books a publisher produces he can be in the business of entertaining, educating, informing, providing escapism or all four.

2.   **Who buys my products or services?**

To continue with our publishing example, students and academics will buy educational textbooks and business books, whereas many diverse groups of people from different socio-economic and ethnic backgrounds, and of varying age groups, will buy non-fiction and fiction novels.

Your organisation might have a wide range of services or products and therefore many different groups of customers. This means that a one fit all solution will not succeed. In order to successfully market to your customers you need to fully understand who they are.

3. What do I know about my target markets?

What is your customers' lifestyle? What do they enjoy doing in their spare time? How do they spend their money? Where do they shop, what are their beliefs, their age, ethnic backgrounds?

And if you are marketing business-to-business what do you know about the industry sector you are targeting? What are the buying patterns? Who is the decision maker? Why would they buy your products?

4. What do your customers want?

Do you understand your customers' needs, their problems, desires and tastes?

5. Where are your customers?

Where do they live? Which area or country?

6. How do you reach them?

What do they read, listen to, or watch on television? Are

they Internet or technologically savvy? Do they attend conferences or exhibitions?

7.   What messages will they respond to?

What sort of images and language would they respond to? How can you persuade them to buy? How can you inform or educate them?

If you have answered all the questions satisfactorily then well done, but you might like to review your answers after reading this book to see if you are on the right track, or if you can improve your marketing further by being more specific in your answers.

Having a clear understanding of your target markets is essential to effective marketing.

The more you know about your customers the easier it will be for you to choose and use the appropriate marketing tool and message to reach them

---

What are the marketing tools?

In order to promote your products/services to your target customers you need to communicate with them in a way they understand and can respond to, which means you need to choose the right marketing method or methods to reach them. These marketing methods or tools include the following:

○ **Advertising**
- television
- radio
- newspapers
- magazines
- directories
- Internet
- wall planners, diaries etc.
- poster advertising e.g. hoardings, billboards railway platforms, bus shelters, buses etc.
- mailshot letters
- leaflets, inserts into magazines and flyers, doordrop leaflets
- 'off the page' advertising
- 'direct response' advertising

○ **Signage**
- business premises
- cars, vans etc.
- uniforms

○ **Promotional items**
- notepads
- pens
- carrier bags
- t-shirts etc.
- giveaways

O **Direct Marketing**
- mail order catalogues
- telemarketing
- e-mail shots/enewsletters
- newsletters
- Internet

O **Editorial**
- news releases

O **Exhibition stands, trade fairs**

O **Personal Selling**
- Selling face to face

O **Seminars/Demonstrations/Open Days**
- inviting your prospects and customers to a seminar, demonstration and open day.

O **Corporate Hospitality**
- inviting prospects and customers to a corporate hospitality event. Your satisfied customers should help you sell to your prospective customers.

O **Sponsorship**
- You can tie this element in with editorial coverage and corporate hospitality.

○ **Sales Promotion Techniques**
  - merchandising – making sure your product is displayed to the maximum effect.
  - giving special offers e.g. two for the price of one, discounts, ten percent extra in order to tempt customers to try the product
  - joint promotions – linking up with other organisations to offer some kind of incentive for customers to buy
  - affiliate marketing – links on web sites with commissions for orders placed
  - loyalty programmes

○ **Personal Recommendations – Word of Mouth**

Choosing the right marketing tools

Before you decide which marketing tools, or mixture of marketing tools to use in order to reach your target markets, there are some further questions you need to ask as well as those I have already previously mentioned. Answering these questions will help you to make the most appropriate choice.

1. What is my objective?

You might think that increasing sales is the only objective and ultimately it is, but there are many roads to this destination, and being more precise in what you are trying to achieve through your marketing campaign/s will help you decide the most effective means of getting there.

For example, is your objective to stimulate orders or enquiries? Are you trying to build your database of potential customers? Are you attempting to build name or brand awareness?

If you are a public sector organisation are you trying to influence the public or educate them? The latter might certainly be the case if, for example, you are running campaigns to help people to stop smoking or to prevent them drinking and driving. If you are a charity then your objective might be to raise money through donations, but you might have other objectives, for example, recruiting trustees or patrons, or educating the public about your cause.

You could have a variety of marketing campaigns running at the same time and to a number of different target audiences. If so, the critical factor for success is to be clear about your objectives

2. Can my message be creatively different and is it the right message?

Each campaign will carry a message to your target customers. Are you clear about this message? How are you going to communicate it through the chosen promotional tool? Will your target customers understand it? Will they respond to it?

3. Will using this promotional tool reach my target audience?

Have you chosen the right marketing tool (or combination of marketing tools) to reach your target customers? For example, it is no good running an advertising campaign in a magazine or newspaper that your target customers are unlikely to read.

> The more you know about your target customers the more successful you will be in reaching them

4. How am I going to follow this through?

People buy what they are familiar with, so you need to keep your company name, and/or your products or services, in front of your target customers on a regular basis. You need to build awareness for your products or services over a period of time.

Many organisations fail in their marketing because:

O   they don't understand what markets they are really in and therefore try to be everything to all people

O   they don't understand why their customers buy from them and therefore don't communicate the right messages

○ they lack consistency in their marketing, flitting from promotional tool to promotional tool not giving any of them time enough to work.

Make sure this doesn't happen to you. Draw up a programme of marketing activity. It doesn't have to be grandiose, simply producing a half yearly newsletter and a news release once a month might be enough. In fact, it might be all you can afford and need. Sending a quarterly mailshot and following it up with a telemarketing campaign and a sales visit might be the right approach for you. Developing an online newsletter and e-mailing your customers regularly might stimulate orders (ensure though that you check out the regulations regarding sending e shots in the country in which you are operating.) A small advertisement in the right magazine once a month combined with a mailshot to certain target customers could bring you results. Or attendance at one or two key exhibitions, with leads being conscientiously followed up with mailshots and telemarketing could work for your organisation.

> The key to successful marketing is consistently sending the right message to the right target audience using the right promotional tools

In the following chapters I will be looking at a variety of marketing tools and how to make them work for your organisation. This book, however, does not cover the selling function i.e. selling by telephone and selling face to face, which requires a high degree of personal development skills and sales training. Information on these two areas are provided in *The Easy Step by Step Guide to Telemarketing, Cold Calling & Appointment Making*, and *The Easy Step by Step Guide to Successful Selling*.

In summary

O understand fully what business you are in and who buys your products or services

O having a clear understanding of your target markets is essential to effective marketing

O the more you know about your customers the easier it will be for you to choose and use the appropriate marketing tool and message to reach them

O in order to promote and sell your goods and services to your target customers you need to communicate with them in a way they understand and can respond to

O before you decide which marketing tools, or mixture of marketing tools to use know your objectives

O the key to successful marketing is consistently sending the right message to the right target audience using the right promotional tools

O people buy what they are familiar with, so you need to keep your company name, and/or your products or services, in front of your target customers on a regular basis.

Chapter 2

Know what your customers are buying

Understanding exactly what your customers are buying will help you send the right message to them.

When people buy they ask themselves the question, 'Why should I? What's in it for me?' They are seeking certain benefits from buying a particular service or product. It is these benefits that you need to communicate strongly in your advertising and promotional campaigns in order to persuade your customers to buy from you.

Benefits and features

> People buy the benefits of a product or
> service not the features

You also need to communicate this in a creative, stimulating, informative and interesting way. This is not easy, which is why good copywriters are in high demand and can command sizeable salaries.

So how do you do this? First, you need to look at the products or services you are offering and identify for each of these the features and benefits.

Here is a simple example to show you what I mean.

Feature		Benefit
A wide range of products	*Which means*	Everything under one roof saving you time and hassle
Easy ordering; buy direct 24/7	*Which means*	It is simple and quick for you to buy, at a time to suit you
Easy access off the motorway with free parking	*Which means*	There are no parking problems, and we are easy to reach and locate, saving you time and hassle
Well established company	*Which means*	You can trust us, we're reliable and experienced, and have many satisfied customers
Free delivery to your door	*Which means*	It is convenient and easy, and it saves you time

The two magic words that turn a feature into a benefit are *which means*

If you are uncertain of the benefits your customers are buying when they purchase goods or services from your organisation then ask them. You can then use some of these comments in your advertising and promotional literature.

It's not just about communicating features and benefits but conveying the right atmosphere or image around the product or service. So we also need to look at why people buy.

People generally buy for two reasons:
Objective reasons
Subjective reasons

Why people buy

Individuals will buy some products or services to satisfy the basic **physiological needs,** that is to satisfy hunger and thirst, to be free from pain or injury; for security or safety reasons, or because they have to comply with the law. These are the **objective reasons** why people buy.

However, it is not always simply a question of needing or wanting a product or service to serve a specific purpose, or to satisfy that basic physiological need that stimulates an individual to buy. For example, there are many headache tablets on the market that can banish pain but how do you make your headache pill stand out from the competition?

The feature of your company's headache pill may be some kind of unique formula; the benefit of this means that the customer's headache will vanish within an instant! But the customer will also be asking other questions about that product before deciding to buy and these will be the **subjective reasons**.

These subjective reasons are personal based and are referred to as the **psychological reasons** involved in buying.

In our headache pill example the customer might be influenced by the trade name, which communicates reliability and reputation. Or a highly respected and well-known medical organisation or doctor might endorse the product. Perhaps the colour of the packaging or the design of the product look reassuring and attracts the customer. Or maybe the product is the most expensive on the market and our customer only wants to be seen to be buying 'the best' for himself or his loved ones. These are the subjective reasons.

The **subjective or psychological reasons for buying a product or a service** can be summed up as follows:

O   to give pleasure

O   to give a sense of satisfaction

O   to feed and raise self esteem

O   to satisfy and feed an ego

○ to reinforce group identity and to give a sense of belonging

○ to satisfy the need for power

○ to satisfy the need for recognition

○ to satisfy the need for approval

○ to satisfy the need for respect

These are some of the aspects that you need to take into consideration when communicating your advertising message.

Promoting a service

A service is intangible. It cannot be seen, touched or tasted like a product. People deliver services and therefore the maxim 'people buy people' is even more relevant and vital here.

So, when people buy a legal service for example, the **objective reasons** are that they need a lawyer to help them resolve a problem.

The subjective reasons are:

○ does this lawyer have an understanding of my situation?

O   does he have the technical expertise to deal with my problem?

O   will I understand what he is telling me?

O   will I be able to contact him when I need to?

O   does this lawyer and law firm have a good reputation?

O   are the staff friendly and helpful?

O   is the lawyer efficient?

O   is the chemistry right between us? Do we get on?

O   can he deal with all my legal matters and therefore save me time?

O   does the lawyer come recommended by my peers?

The advertising messages here then must not only communicate features and benefits but also convey some or all of the above.

In summary

○ understanding exactly what your customers are buying will help you send the right message to them

○ when people buy they ask themselves the question, 'What's in it for me?'

○ you need to communicate the benefits of your products/services in your advertising and promotional campaigns

○ the two magic words that turn a feature into a benefit are *which means*

○ people generally buy for two reasons: objective and subjective reasons

○ individuals will buy some products or services to satisfy the basic **physiological needs**. These are the **objective reasons** why people buy

○ the **subjective reasons** are personal based and are referred to as the **psychological reasons** involved in buying.

Chapter 3

The market place and marketing planning

So you know who your customers are, and you know your products and services, but how do you plan what marketing activity to undertake?

Part of your marketing involves you taking a look at your business and analysing its strengths and weaknesses. It also involves you looking at the market place in which your business operates and examining the opportunities and threats.

This is called carrying out a SWOT analysis.

SWOT analysis

The SWOT analysis should be conducted at least twice yearly and your marketing plan should address the weaknesses in your business and build on the strengths you have identified. It should also state how you are going to capitalize on the opportunities and what action you are going to take to overcome any threats to the business.

The strengths and weaknesses focus on the **internal** aspects of your business; the opportunities and threats the **external**, and therefore to a certain degree are outside your control; they cover the political, environmental, social and technological activities in the outside world that have an impact on a business.

An example SWOT could look like this:

Strengths	Weaknesses
Good customer base	Weak on developing new products for customers
Good product range	Web site out of date
Well motivated staff	Reception area needs updating
Opportunities	**Threats**
Growth in older population creating new opportunities for us	Higher interest rates could affect consumer spending
Internet use increasing therefore opening up possible new markets for us	Change of government could affect legislation in our markets
Some competitors closing down	New competitors entering market

You need to be aware of what is happening in your market place now, and possibly in the future, which could affect your business? What action do you need to take as a result of this?

The same item could appear under both columns. For example, legislation introduced by the government could pose both a threat and an opportunity to your organisation. The competition could also be both a threat and an opportunity i.e. you might be able to take market share from your competitors, but equally they could take market share from you.

Other things that need to be considered under these headings are:

O   **Consumer attitudes, changing lifestyles, habits, values and trends**

How will these affect your business? Identifying gaps in the market for new products and services could spring from being attuned to changing consumer patterns. Our lifestyle today is much faster than that of previous generations. Customers want their products delivered quickly, hence the growth of same day delivery services. Those organisations that spot the opportunities presented by changing consumer attitudes will continue to gain a competitive advantage and win market share.

O   **Technological developments**

How will technology impact on your business? Digital television is set to open up new markets and change buying habits. E-commerce is a reality. Can your organisation embrace it and exploit it as an opportunity to reach new markets or are your competitors leaving you behind? How will technology change the way your business operates? How will it change the way your customers choose a supplier or buy goods?

O   **Legislation**

Perhaps new legislation will open up a new market for you, but it could also seriously affect the viability of a business and its markets.

O   **Economic**

Recession, recovery, interest rate increases or decreases. How much money do people or businesses have to spend or invest? How will this affect your company's performance?

The marketing action plan

So to recap:

Identify your target markets

Divide your existing and potential customers into easily identifiable groups. Understand who your customers are, where they are, what they buy, why they buy, how much and when. What value do they put on your products or services? What markets are you really in?

Identify your services/products

What is the range of products or services on offer? Is this the right mix for your target customers? Are you continually looking at developing new products/services for your customers and new markets? Are you always seeking to improve your products/services? What are the features and benefits of the products/services you offer?

Know your competitors

Where are you in the market place in relation to your competitors? What are your competitors' strengths and weaknesses? What is your brand share, market share? What are your competitors' prices, and sales strategies? What new products or services are they developing? How do you compare to them?

Conduct a SWOT Analysis

Identify the strengths and weaknesses within your organisation. Say what you are going to do to build on the strengths and eliminate the weaknesses. Identify the external opportunities and threats.

Set your marketing objectives

Most marketing plans run for a year at a time but it is a good idea to set, or at least have some idea of your broad objectives in the longer term, say three to five years. A word of caution though, it is becoming increasingly difficult to plan very far ahead as the pace of change today is so fast, and the introduction of new technology is daily re-writing the text books on business operation and business development. Having said that, however, you still need to set objectives at least on an annual basis.

When setting your objectives it is not enough to say that you want to be the best company in town because how are you going to measure that? How do you know when you are the best?

Your objectives therefore have to be specific and measurable. In short they need to be **S.M.A.R.T**.

S.M.A.R.T. stands for

Specific
Measurable
Achievable
Realistic
Timed

Here are some example objectives:

O To increase market share of x product/service from 10% to 20% of the current market by January 200X

O To increase sales of x product/service from £1.8m to £2m by January 200X

O To maintain % profitability levels on x product range over the year

O To investigate at least two new markets and to identify one key market to penetrate in 200X

Whatever your objectives ensure they are realistic and achievable. If you set them too high, or have too many, then they will be difficult to achieve and this only becomes demotivating.

Marketing strategies

So, how are you going to achieve your marketing objectives? How are you going to increase sales, increase your customer base, build profitability etc.?

There are four basic marketing strategies; these are:

1. Market Penetration
This involves keeping your existing customers and finding new ones.

2. Product or Service Development
This involves improving your existing products or services i.e. improving the quality, adapting the style, offering something new for your existing customers.

3. Market Extension
This involves finding new markets for your existing products or services i.e. going further afield geographically, or appealing to a new group or type of customers.

4. Diversification
This involves increasing your sales by developing new products for new markets.

This final strategy carries the highest cost and the highest risk. You are entering a market you know nothing about, with a product or service you have no experience of. Businesses usually adopt a combination of the first three strategies to achieve their objectives.

You then need to develop a marketing action plan for each strategy to help you achieve your objectives. You might have a marketing action plan for each target group of customers and/or for each product or service supplied, which brings me on to choosing the right promotional tools to use in your marketing action plan to achieve the objectives you have set. The following chapters examine the promotional tools and how you can use them.

In summary

○ a SWOT analysis should be conducted twice yearly. This looks at the internal strengths and weaknesses of your business and the external opportunities and threats

○ marketing objectives should be **S.M.A.R.T.**
This stands for:
Specific
Measurable
Achievable
Realistic
Timed

○ don't set too many objectives. If you can't fulfill them you will become de-motivated

○ there are four basic marketing strategies to help you achieve your objectives. These are:
- Market Penetration
- Product/Service Development
- Market Extension
- Diversification

○ you need to develop a marketing action plan to help you achieve your objectives.

Chapter 4

Advertising

Advertising doesn't just apply to taking space in a newspaper or magazine, or running a campaign on the radio and television, as I listed in chapter one it covers a number of different areas. Let me recap.

○ **Advertising**
- television
- radio
- newspapers
- magazines
- directories
- Internet
- wall planners, diaries etc.
- poster advertising e.g. hoardings, railway platforms, bus shelters, buses etc.
- mailshot letters
- leaflets, inserts into magazines and flyers, doordrop leaflets
- 'off the page' advertising
- 'direct response' advertising

○ **Signage**
- business premises
- cars, vans etc.
- uniforms

O   **Promotional items**
     - notepads
     - pens
     - carrier bags
     - t-shirts etc.
     - giveaways

Before deciding whether or not to advertise in any of these areas you need to address the questions that I posed in chapter one, namely:

1.   What is your objective?
2.   Who are you targeting?
3.   Will this form of advertising reach them?
4.   Is advertising something they would respond to?
5.   How can my message be creatively different?

Advertising Objectives

Listed below are some objectives for advertising:

O   to build demand for your product or service on launch

O   to give the customer details and instructions on how to use a product

O   to build brand recognition for your product

O   to create a certain image for the brand, or for the company

○ to give information about a price promotion and so stimulate demand

○ to build names and addresses on the database

○ to educate people e.g. drink driving campaigns, no smoking campaigns

○ to back up sales drives

○ to drive visitors to your web site

○ to influence consumers to buy.

Before you advertise you will also need to know the answers to the following questions:

○ who buys your product or service?

○ why do they buy it?

○ what is it used for?

○ what is the extent of advertising needed to reach that target group of customers?

○ how much do you need to do to get the message across?

Plus:

○ What media are my target customers exposed to?

○ What do I know about the media?

Advertising media

Printed media: magazines, newspapers, directories, wall planners, diaries

If you decide to advertise in a printed publication then always obtain a copy of it beforehand, or look up the details on the Internet where the majority of publications now have a presence. If, however, you are advertising in a local directory, on a wall planner, or something similar, then there might not be an appropriate web site giving you details of the publication, in this case ask to see a copy of a previous publication before you decide whether or not to advertise. You also need to ask yourself the following questions:

○ does this publication look like the kind of thing that would attract my customers?

○ who else is advertising in it?

○ are any of my competitors advertising and if so does this mean we should?

○ are there complimentary products and services on offer? You could try telephoning a couple of the advertisers (but probably not your competitors) to ask about their response

○ what is the content of the editorial, (if any), and would it appeal to my target customers?

O   would my target customers buy/read/use/see
        this publication?

O   what are the circulation figures and the
        readership? (You might be able to view this on
        the publication's web site.)

O   how often is the magazine/newspaper/
        directory/wall planner published?

O   what are the rates, the copy deadlines and what
        special deals will they do for me?

Is it only advertising in the printed publication that
appeals to you or should you be considering teaming
this up with online advertising on the publication's
web site? This could be effective, depending on the
publication and your target audience, because there
might be a group of customers who only read online,
another who prefers to have the printed version in their
hands and a third that view both.

In order to obtain costs and relevant information about a
publication you should be able to download a media pack
from the advertiser's web site (unless you are dealing
with very small and localised publications, in which case
ask them for full costs and readership figures).

In addition, does the publication have a feature list and
does this fit with your products and services? If so you
might wish to consider advertising around a special
feature, or seeing if you could get some editorial into

the publication during that feature. Most media packs and publications' web sites provide details of their core target audience, which will help you to match it against your target customers.

Broadcast media

Check if this is the right media for your products and services. Ask the radio or television station for audience figures, and how far their audience reaches. Obtain information about the programme's type of audience, for example their age and socio economic background. Who listens to, or watches, that programme, are they your target audience? When and how do they listen to the radio station? For example, is this in the car on their way to and from work, or at work or home? What time of day do they listen?

Who else is advertising on that radio station or television channel? Are they your competitors or do their products/ services fit well with yours? What is the cost of advertising including the cost of producing the advertisement, and how long will you need to run the campaign in order to get your target audience to respond?

Poster advertising: hoardings, railway station platforms, bus shelters, buses, ad vans and mobile billboards

Poster and billboard advertising doesn't have to be national; you can tailor this to where your customers are based. Most poster advertising is handled by specialist companies, or advertising and marketing agencies. They will be able to search for the best providers of these services, and negotiate space and cost on your behalf. They will also be able to design a poster, or series of posters, and advise on how best to get your message across.

Alternatively you can search for companies on the Internet who specialise in this area, who will provide you with information on locations, poster production and costs.

Are there any other places where you might legitimately be able to advertise your organisation? Think about your product/service and target customers, where do they visit, drive? What do they see? Are there opportunities to advertise, or to place a sign in that location?

We now have advertising in a variety of locations and some unusual places. For example, in Britain, advertisements can be found on roundabouts and on the back of toilet doors in motorway service stations. I've even seen adverts on a herd of cows in a field beside a motorway!

Internet advertising

There are a huge number of Internet sites advertising and selling goods and services. The advent of Broadband technology and the ability to access web sites through mobile communications and wireless technology has made this a truly mobile, flexible and cost effective way to market goods.

You can advertise your products/services on your web site, as well as with search engines like Google. You might also consider joining affiliate programmes to advertise other companies' products and services on your web site and vice versa, and generate revenue when visitors click through from your site to the affiliate web site.

Remember though that the same rules that apply to other forms of advertising also apply to electronic advertising in that it is unfair, illegal and unethical to deceive customers and misrepresent services and goods.

'Off the Page' advertising

'Off the page' advertisements appear in many magazines and newspapers. Customers can buy the product 'off the page' paying by cheque or credit card, either by using the coupon response or by telephoning to place their order. Here, then, you need to display your product advert in the most appropriate publication i.e. one that reaches your target customers. You might also wish to consider outsourcing fulfilment to a specialist company if you expect the response to be high, or if you do not have adequate in house resources to handle it.

Direct response advertising

Many products and services are sold direct through advertising on the television or radio. Often a free phone telephone number, or low cost number, is provided. Charities cost effectively raise thousands of pounds through their direct response advertising campaigns targeted at key times throughout the year, for example at Christmas. With direct response advertising the customer calls the telephone number given and pays for the product via a credit or debit card. You need to match carefully your target customer with the target media. You will also need to ensure that your organisation, or the outsourced call centre, can handle the response to a campaign.

Mailshot letters, leaflets, inserts into magazines and flyers, doordrop leaflets

This type of advertising is generally known as **direct marketing** because you are communicating with your audience direct rather than through an intermediary. However, when writing and designing a mailshot campaign including letters, leaflets, door drops and inserts into magazines and newspapers, the rules of good advertising apply, which is why I have included it here. Those rules of good advertising are covered in the following chapter. Well-targeted and well-designed mailshots, tailored and personalised to the customer, can be an extremely successful form of marketing. They are controllable and the results can be measured.

Signage: business premises, vehicles, uniforms

Don't overlook the opportunity to boost your organisation's profile through obvious signage like that stated above. Of course this is not relevant to every business, but signage and uniforms are a positive marketing tool when it comes to marketing a service, helping to reinforce brand identity and image. If you are advertising on your company vehicles consider the image and impression your drivers are making on the public. A cleaning company with dirty vans is not a good advertisement, and reckless and rude drivers can severely damage an organisation's reputation and therefore lose vital sales.

E shots

These are a direct form of marketing, where you are targeting customers direct. As with direct mail it is best that you check out the rules and regulations regarding the sending of e shots in your country before embarking on a campaign because different countries have different legislation covering this. For full information on e-mail marketing see chapters six and seven.

Promotional items: notepads, pens, carrier bags, t-shirts, giveaways

Promoting your organisation's name and key marketing message through certain promotional items that are often given away for free can help to spread the word and reinforce brand name and image. They won't stimulate sales on their own, but coupled with other marketing activity they could help to keep your organisation's name in front of your target customers on an ongoing basis.

Whichever media you choose, ensure that all the media details match with your target audience. Be clear about your objectives for advertising. How to make your advertising more effective is covered in the following chapters.

In summary

○   before deciding whether or not to advertise you
need to be clear:
- about your objective
- who you are targeting
- whether the chosen form of advertising will
reach your target customers
- would they respond to it?
- how your message can be creatively different?

Chapter 5

How to make advertising and mailshots work

In order to be effective, advertising (wherever this might be including direct mail) must create a sense of familiarity with the target audience.

In order to work adverts and direct mail must be:

Seen
Read
Remembered
Believed
Acted upon

Successful advertising also needs to fulfil the following criteria:

The customer must be aware of the brand or company

In order to build awareness you need to advertise over a period of time, and/or advertise in a number of different media at the same time. Alternatively, you might mix your promotional tools, for example whilst running an advertising campaign in a publication your target audience reads, you might also run a direct mail campaign, coupled with some editorial in relevant magazines, so that the prospect becomes more aware of your company/brand across a range of media to which they are exposed.

There must be some *understanding* of what the product is and what it will do for the customer

This means that your message must explain clearly and succinctly how buying the product/brand/service will benefit the customer.

The customer must arrive at the mental *conviction* to buy the product

Your message must also carry a genuine attractiveness that convinces the customer he must have it, so a clear understanding of what your customer wants is paramount.

The customer must stir himself into *action*

You need to get the customer saying, *'Yes, I must have that.'* And you need to make it easy for him to buy.

Advertising regulations

Advertising and direct mailing regulations can vary from country to country so always make sure that you comply with the law. In some countries advertising is very prominent, whilst in others it is practically non-existent. So, again, it is a question of understanding your target audience and knowing the best methods to reach them. In addition, certain products may be banned from being advertised, like cigarettes in the UK. And there is, of course, the question of advertising in the language of the country, does your product name and advertising message need to change to make sense and appeal to the right people?

Making your advertising message work

As I mentioned before, to make your advertising work it needs to be seen, read, remembered, believed and acted upon. So how do you do this? The answer is by conforming to **AIDA**. This stands for:

A	=	**Attention**
I	=	**Interest**
D	=	**Desire**
A	=	**Action**

This very simple rule also applies to making your direct mail letters, leaflets, brochures and inserts more effective.

Attention

> You need to grab the **ATTENTION**

You have only a couple of seconds to catch someone's attention before they turn the page, put your mailshot in the waste paper bin, switch off the radio, flick channels on the television, see your poster advert or turn the page of a magazine. So you need to make sure that you grab their attention.

To do this you need to be imaginative. Here are some techniques to help you.

Try using a strong headline or a bold question, something that captures or plays on your key benefit. Remember our features and benefits exercise? It is the benefits that persuade people to buy, not the features.

On television and the Internet, you can use a number of techniques to capture the imagination. Television, cinema and the Internet use moving pictures with sound and vision both of which you can exploit, but that doesn't necessarily mean people will keep watching, they may zap channels, or pop out to make a drink, or buy an ice cream, or click off your web site if it is too slow to load, therefore missing your expensive advertisement.

Again, you need to think of your target audience, what messages and images would they respond to: humour, horror, shock, sex, cartoons or nostalgia?

You can also use sound effects to grab attention. Loud music, familiar music, contrast in style and levels of music, a catchy jingle, an unusual sound or a good voiceover artist can all work.

In the printed media you can use colour to make your advertisement stand out in a black and white publication. Or you could use a black or coloured border. Borders are very effective. Illustrations or photographs also work well. Or you could use a combination of the above. But **don't** fall into the trap of trying to cram too much text into too small a space. There is some truth in the maxim; the less said the better, certainly when it comes to advertisements.

> Use white space; it will help your
> advertisement to stand out

Keep it simple. Too much text and your advertisement will be lost in all the other text on the page.

Look through the advertisements in magazines and newspapers to see which ones stand out. Ask yourself why and then adapt the technique to suit your own advertisements.

A mailshot letter or leaflet should begin with a bold statement or question, and should contain a key benefit first. In the letter this is usually presented in bold and goes under the salutation and before the body copy of the letter.

Don't begin a mailshot letter with waffle, or with the standard, 'I am writing to introduce my company to you.' It's obvious you are writing, and besides I didn't invite you to introduce your company to me, did I?

If you don't make your letter easy to read then why should your reader bother with it? You haven't got time to wade through lots of text searching for the benefits so don't insult your reader by thinking that he isn't as busy as you are.

Interest

> Stimulate **INTEREST**

Here, we return to our features and benefits exercise. What are the other benefits you are offering? Make these benefits strong in your advertising copy, mailshot letter and leaflet, to add conviction.

When writing the copy always remember your target audience, what language do they speak? What will they respond to?

In a mailshot letter address the recipient direct i.e. Dear Mr Smith, not Dear sir, or Dear householder. Use short words, short sentences and short paragraphs. Use YOU and I instead of WE. Remember you are trying to create the impression of writing to the customer personally so make it user-friendly. Use frequent sub headings or bullet points to break up copy. Be clear, straightforward, uncluttered and avoid jargon. Be as natural as you can, as if you are having a conversation with the person.

Always consider the reader's needs, in your advertisement, leaflet, flyer or letter. Make sure you interest him by giving benefits.

> Remember people always ask *'what's in it for me?'* Address this question in your advertisements, and mailshots. Tell them what's in it for them

Develop interest with the best benefit and win them over with second and further benefits. Follow your copy through from the heading. You must get the reader saying, *'Yes, I must have some of that!'* And there must be something in the letter, leaflet or advertisement for the reader wherever he looks.

Make it easy for the reader (or listener if on radio) to understand what the offer is. They shouldn't have to spend hours fathoming it out, and of course they won't.

Having gained interest you then need to inspire desire.

Desire

> Inspire **DESIRE**

Here you need to strengthen the benefits of your product/service. You can use questions to hold the interest and build desire.

Be enthusiastic. Be friendly. Be helpful. Revisit your features and benefits. Add in the features that would appeal to the target customers and emphasise the benefits of these, for example, free car parking; a free quotation; money back guarantee; an accessible location; friendly, helpful, expert staff; long and convenient opening hours, or an easy way of ordering.

Make your target customers really want what you are offering.

Action

> Finally prompt **ACTION**

Enclose a coupon or a fax back reply. Provide an e-mail and web site address. Tell the customer he can get further information by clicking onto your web site.

Let your customer tick boxes rather than having to fill in forms; people find it easier and quicker.

Give an incentive for your customers to take action, use a free trial, free consultation, free brochure or possibly a free gift.

> Remember A.I.D.A.
>
> Attention – Interest – Desire - Action

More about mailshots

Well-targeted and well-designed mailshots can be an extremely successful form of marketing. They are controllable and the results can be measured. We have already looked at the golden rules for writing mailshot letters and leaflets, but there are some additional rules you'd do well to remember to ensure your mailings don't become junk mail.

Secrets of a Good Mailshot

O   **The mailing list**

This must be as accurate as possible and up to date. The mailshot must be targeted to the right person and must be sent to a named individual.

O   **The product/service and the offer**

There must be something in the mailshot for the reader – a strong offer and clear benefits.

O   **The sender must have an affinity with the receiver**

You must communicate the right message. In order to be successful you must talk the language of your target customers.

O   **A response mechanism**

You must make it easy for the reader to respond. Give him a coupon to complete and post, or a fax back. Or refer them to your web site. Make your telephone number bold to encourage him to pick up the phone to you. In addition, freepost and a free telephone numbers can help to lift response.

O   **Plan for a campaign**

As I have already said one off advertisements and mailshots rarely achieve much. Don't bombard people though, but plan a mailshot perhaps once a quarter or three times a year whichever might be relevant and suitable for your products/services and the industry or consumers you are targeting.

In summary

○   in order to be effective, advertising must create a sense of familiarity with the target audience

○   people buy what they know and recognise

○   advertisements over a period of time raise awareness and build credibility

○   in order to work adverts and direct mail must be:
- Seen
- Read
- Remembered
- Believed
- Acted upon

○   the customer must be *aware* of the brand or company

○   there must be some *understanding* of what the product is and what it will do for the customer

○   the customer must arrive at the mental *conviction* to buy the product

○   the customer must stir himself into *action*

○   Your advertising message should conform to
    AIDA:
    - **A**   =   **Attention**
    - **I**   =   **Interest**
    - **D**   =   **Desire**
    - **A**   =   **Action**

○   well-targeted and well-designed mailshots can
    be an extremely successful form of marketing.

Chapter 6

E-mail marketing

Different countries have different legislation regarding the sending of unsolicited e-mails so it is always best to check out the legislation in the country you are targeting before embarking on a campaign.

In the UK this legislation is covered by the Privacy in Electronic Communications Directive and the Regulations define electronic mail as:

'any text, voice, sound or image message sent over a public electronic communications network which can be stored in the network or in the recipient's terminal equipment until it is collected by the recipient and includes messages sent using a short message service.'

Messages using Bluetooth technology and sent to all Bluetooth enable handsets are also considered to be 'electronic mail.'

What you can and can't do – business to consumer marketing

Individuals are defined as a residential subscriber or a sole trader for a non limited liability partnership who would use an e-mail address that would look something like the following example: joebloggs@hotmail.com.

In the UK all e-mail marketing to individuals must be done with their express permission; they must **'opt in'**.

There is an exception however, which is called the **'soft opt in'** rule. This is where you can send a marketing e-mail to an individual subscriber without their consent only if you comply with the following rules:

1. you must have obtained the contact details of this person in the course of a sale or negotiation, or in the course of the sale of a product or service

and

2. the marketing information you are sending relates to similar services and products

and

3. the recipient has been given a simple means of refusing the use of his contact details for marketing purposes at the time those details were initially collected

and

4. where he did not refuse the use of the details, at the time of each subsequent communication.

If you satisfy these criteria you do not need prior consent to send marketing by e-mail to individual subscribers.

If collecting e-mails, or mobile phone numbers, as part of a competition or promotion then make sure you ask the customer if you can use this information to communicate with him in this way on future offers and promotions. If you collect his details and do not make it clear that you would like to contact him by e-mail with further offers in the future then you will breach the regulations.

Buying in or renting a list from a third party

If you buy in, or rent a list from a third party, you can only use it if it was obtained by that third party on a clear **prior consent** basis, that is where the intended recipient has actively consented to receiving unsolicited e-mails messages from a third party.

Always seek assurance that the list you are buying or renting has followed the requirements of the law. The third party selling or renting the list must have obtained consent from the customer through the use of a clause. For example if the third party is a gardening company that subsequently sells or rents its list to other gardening companies then it should have used a clause like the following:

O   I am happy to hear from other companies that offer gardening products. Please pass my details onto them so that they contact me.

Or they might have used a clause that is unspecified for example:

O   I want to hear from other companies about their online offers. Please pass my details onto them.

However, before e-mailing the customer you should always check your own database to make sure the person has not already sent an 'opt out' request to you.

Do not conceal your identity when you contact them and make sure you provide them with a valid contact address for subsequent 'opt outs.'

As with mailshots the same applies to e shots in that the older the list the less likely the recipient is to respond positively to a marketing message, and the more likely you are to have waste. It might even damage your organisation's reputation if you send poorly targeted marketing messages to individuals who are no longer interested in those services and products.

The best lists are ones that you have built yourself. Make sure that all your staffs capture e-mail addresses and that they ask permission to contact the prospect or customer by e-mail and send them relevant information. You might also wish to run a telemarketing campaign to build an e-mail list, or a direct marketing campaign to capture e-mail addresses, perhaps referring people to your web site where they can register for updates or your enewsletter, or obtain free information (see Chapter Seven on enewsletters).

Offer an incentive that you can fulfil electronically, for example a free report or fact sheet that can be downloaded from your web site.

Keep the data clean, personalise messages as much as you can to avoid them looking and sounding like spam. Don't bombard people with messages. Once a month or every six weeks is enough.

What you can and can't do - business to business marketing

In the UK you can send a marketing e-mail to those you have on your database without needing to gain their permission first. You must not, however, conceal your identity when you send a marketing message and you must provide a valid address to which the recipient can send an 'opt out' request if he so wishes.

Ask your customers how they prefer to be contacted. This will not only help you to tailor campaigns by sending them the right message in the right way, but will also save you money, and even prevent you from falling foul of the law and incurring penalties. A simple question on correspondence will suffice, for example:

Please contact me by :

O   Post
O   Telephone
O   Text
O   E-mail with further information about your
         products and services

Try and aim for permission-based marketing as much as you can, provide a statement of use when you collect details from customer and put this somewhere visible, so that customers can easily read it. Make it easy for customers to 'opt out' and comply with their requests promptly.

Because people often have more than one e-mail address it might be advisable to include the recipient's e-mail address in the message and a line that says, 'click here to remove xyz@acme.com' that way the recipient can see which e-mail address is being deleted.

Of course, this regulation does not prevent UK citizens receiving unsolicited e-mail and text messages sent from other countries where the laws are more lenient or non existent.

You can obtain comprehensive and useful advice about this area of marketing from the following web site *www.ico.gov.uk* or call the Information Commissioner's Office Helpline 01625 545745.

Is it worth it? – Does e-mail marketing work?

After reading the above I wouldn't blame you if you were thinking should I bother? Does e-mail marketing work, especially given the amount that we all have to cope with today, and the spam that we continually receive? Well, the quick answer to that is yes, it can work, but I am acutely aware that anything that concerns the Internet and technology can be relevant one day and practically extinct the next.

The way, therefore, to make your marketing more effective is not just to consider one method of reaching your customers but several. And, of course, you will not be sending them e-mail marketing messages if they do not wish to receive them.

Your campaigns might consist of telemarketing the customer or prospective customer, sending direct mail and following up with electronic mail. Or it might be sending an e-mail and then following up with a letter, or phone call.

Benefits of an e-mail campaign

The major benefits of an e-mail campaign are:

O   it is quick, simple and highly cost effective

O   it can be personalised

O   click throughs can be tracked and responses measured

O   the ability to click on a link to a web site is a great asset.

How to make your e-mail marketing more effective

Build a list

In house lists usually generate the best response so build a list of your customers both old and new. If you don't have their e-mail addresses then you might wish to run a telemarketing campaign to capture them, but ensure you explain exactly why you want the e-mail address, and how you will be using it. If the customer doesn't wish to give you permission to contact him with promotional offers by e-mail then he has the right to do so.

Writing e-mail copy

Subject heading

You have about three seconds to get the recipient's attention before he decides to read it or delete it. Be short and to the point, give him a reason to open the mail, grab his attention but don't make it too gimmicky or it could look like spam. It should be clear from the subject header what the e-mail is about. Think about your offer and your target customers, also your key benefit. Subject lines should be no more than about five to eight words.

Think of the subject line as one sentence that can summarise your campaign. Not easy I know, but essential. Be clear and concise.

Make it chatty

E-mails are more natural in their style of communication than formal. Make it chatty in the right tone of voice to suit your target audience. Read it aloud, how does it sound? E-mail must sound personal to that customer even though you are targeting many. Check your spelling, punctuation and grammar.

Use language that communicates directly on a one to one basis; don't let it look like spam. Don't use the word 'free', or capitals and lots of exclamation marks, it will look tacky. If you can, personalise it with the information you have about that customer or group of customers.

Keep it brief

Once again you are trying to satisfy that basic question the customer is asking himself i.e. 'What's in it for me?' Why should the recipient read the e-mail and why would he be interested in what you have to offer?

The first couple of lines are critical. Short simple sentences and clarity is vital. Like the direct mail letter it will be scanned before it is read properly, so you have only a short space of time to capture and hold attention.

Lead your customers to your web site for further details and benefits and where they can have the opportunity to contact you. A simple landing page will give you extra space for you to convince them.

Don't try to do it all in one hit

Like most other forms of marketing, it takes time to build awareness and communicate a message. Remember back to chapter five, your messages need to be seen, read, remembered, believed, and then acted upon. E-mail marketing is not a one hit wonder, think of it as a long term communicating process.

Testing it

Come up with a couple of different styles of e-mail messages and send them as test messages either back to yourself to see what they look like in your in box, or to a number of people in your company, or even to one or two 'tame' customers. Test it on a small sample of people and if it works roll it out.

The most successful e-mail campaigns are those that build on responses. Like all marketing, people buy what they are familiar with so keep the continuity going.

Viral marketing

This is a term used to increase brand awareness or word of mouth through the Internet. It uses pre-existing social networks to spread 'word of mouth' online. It can also use blogs to spread the word. A 'blog' is an online diary where others can post comments on what you have said and refer you on to other web sites.

Viral marketing means that people will pass on and share interesting or funny content and so create an awareness and even demand for the product or brand. It is cheaper than direct mail and avoids spam because only friends send to friends. It can reach a wide number of people very rapidly.

Often the goal of viral marketing is to generate media coverage via offbeat stories.

Viral advertising is where people will pass on and share entertaining content, and is often sponsored by a brand looking to build awareness for a product or service. This usually takes the form of video clips or games and images, and can include text.

In summary

○ check out the legislation in the country you are targeting before embarking on a campaign.

○ In the UK all e-mail marketing to individuals must be done with their express permission; they must **'opt in'**

○ there is an exception however – the **'soft opt in'** rule

○ make sure you ask the customer if you can use his e-mail address to communicate with him in this way

○ if you buy in, or rent a list from a third party, you can only use it if it was obtained by that third party on a clear **prior consent** basis

○ do not conceal your identity when you contact the customer by e-mail

○ provide a valid contact address for subsequent 'opt outs'

○ the older the list the less likely the recipient is to respond positively to a marketing message

○ the best lists are ones that you build yourself

○ keep the data clean, personalise messages

O   you can send a marketing e-mail to those businesses you have on your database without needing to gain their permission first

O   ask your customers how they prefer to be contacted

O   provide a statement of use when you collect details and put this somewhere visible, so that customers can easily read it

O   when writing e-mail copy be short and to the point; give him a reason to open the mail

O   use language that communicates directly on a one to one basis; don't let it look like spam

O   lead your customers to your web site for further details and benefits

O   test it.

Chapter 7

Newsletters and eNewsletters

Producing regular and content specific newsletters is a very effective marketing tool both the printed version and the enewsletter. They can keep your existing customers and target customers informed of new products and services, and they help to keep your company name in front of your customers on a regular basis. They build credibility and engender a feeling of trust.

In order to work however, newsletters must be produced regularly. They are not an easy option, and it takes time and effort to produce them and build a good a subscriber base.

The first step in launching a successful newsletter is to be clear about your objectives. You will also need to know your target audience. Only then can you provide them with information that they want. If your customers are extremely diverse then perhaps you should consider developing more than one newsletter or enewsletter and tailoring the information to suit that particular group of customers. Alternatively you could tailor the front and back pages, but keep the content inside the newsletter the same for each group of customers. Not that your newsletter has to be four pages, it can easily be a two page double-sided affair.

Your existing customers are the obvious starting point for subscribers to your newsletter, but you will also be keen to add new prospects to this list, to build a dialogue with them over time and boost your chances of winning new business from them. So, how can you build a subscription list?

Building a subscription list

○ Position subscription details on your web site

○ Offer an incentive for your customers to subscribe, perhaps they can obtain a free guide or information

○ Make sure that information about your newsletters and enewsletters are in your company brochures and leaflets along with information telling the customer how he can subscribe

○ Send a press release to your local, regional and trade press, launching the newsletter or enewsletter and add in the launch issue some useful advice that potential subscribers need

○ Invite a subscription with every e-mail you send linked into your signature, and don't forget to add the link to your web site

○ Remind subscribers to forward the enewsletter to their contacts or friends and so help to spread the word (viral marketing)

O Make sure that everyone in your company knows about the newsletter and/or enewsletter and that they tell new and prospective customers about it.

Content is critical

Newsletters and enewsletters are not company puff and they are not the hard sell. They must have information of real value to the subscriber. You also need to make your newsletter stand out from others. You want your subscribers to look forward to receiving the newsletter. At least eighty percent of the information should be meaty content written in an editorial style. Give them news, information and advice, not what you think you should sell them. Put yourself in the shoes of your target customers and think about what they would like to read. Content can include interviews, case studies, snippets of news, fun articles, FAQs. For more information on this topic you might like to read our sister publication *The Easy Step by Step Guide to Writing Newsletters and Articles*.

Consistency and timing

Developing a personality for your newsletter will help it stand out from the competition. Also consistency is critical. Make sure you draw up a publication timetable and stick to it – no excuses that you were too busy to bring out the summer edition. If you skip an issue your customers/subscribers will feel they can no longer rely on you, and you also break that loyalty chain you are trying to forge. How often you issue your newsletter depends on how much you have to say and your target audience. Enewsletters tend to come out with more frequency than the printed newsletters. You may wish to issue an enewsletter once a month, and a printed version once a quarter. You don't have to issue both but can do either. However, whatever you decide be realistic about whether or not it is achievable for you. Don't promise something you can't deliver.

Customer feedback

Encourage customer feedback. This can be done through a competition or invite them to post a comment or join a forum on your web site.

Develop a questionnaire to get feedback on your organisation's products or services. Send this out with your newsletter, or put a click through on your enewsletter. Offer to enter responses into a free prize draw, or provide a discount or a money-off voucher for their next purchase.

In summary

O   newsletters are a very effective marketing tool.
     They can keep both your existing customers
     and target customers informed of new products
     and services

O   they help to keep your company name in front
     of your customers on a regular basis

O   they build credibility and engender a feeling of
     trust

O   they must be produced regularly

O   be clear about your objectives and know your
     target audience

O   position subscription details on your web site

O   offer an incentive for your customers to
     subscribe

O   ensure that information about your
     newsletters and enewsletters are in your
     company brochures

O   send a press release to your local, regional
     and trade press, launching the newsletter or
     enewsletter

O   invite a subscription with every e-mail you
    send linked into your signature, and don't
    forget to add a link to your web site

O   remind subscribers to forward the enewsletter
    to their contacts or friends

O   newsletters should contain information of value

O   draw up a publication timetable and stick to it

O   include a questionnaire to get customer
    feedback on your products/services.

Chapter 8

Corporate brochures and web sites

Corporate brochures

Do you need a corporate brochure? What are you going to do with it when you get it? I have been to many organisations where the corporate brochure has cost them the earth and yet it sits in the bottom of a cupboard collecting dust. I have even had people say to me that their brochure is too expensive for them to send out – what was the point of producing it then!!

First, ask yourself why you need a brochure. Is it to be mailed to people on request? Is it to be displayed in reception? To be taken to an exhibition or for use by the sales force? Or are you going to use it for all of these things and more. If you wish to use it as a mailing tool then perhaps you would be better off designing a direct mail leaflet.

Second, ask who your brochure is aimed at? Who are you trying to communicate with? If you have a wide cross section of target audiences then you might need several brochures to communicate with them because each group of customers will talk a different language.

What special, unique selling points or benefits are you going to emphasise in your brochure? What corporate image are you trying to portray? What is the personality of your company and how can this be communicated in your brochure? Does the brochure need photographs or illustrations? Should it be full colour, one colour or two? What size should it be?

In addition, try not to have too many people involved in the design of a corporate brochure, because they will all have different views about what they like. The end result can be that you end up with something that looks as though it's been designed by a committee, and the essential message and image will have been diluted, or even lost completely. Remember it is not what you would like in a brochure but what your target audience would like.

And, of course, look at your budget. Corporate brochures can be expensive. Make sure you spend your money wisely on a brochure that serves its purpose, and one that will work for you and reach the right target audience.

When writing for a corporate brochure you will need to decide what essential information should be included. Does it have to explain the complete range of products or services or only some of them? Is it going to be a teaser brochure? By that I mean portraying the company image and core message without giving in depth details about the services or products. Whatever it includes though remember to stress the benefits of the customer using or contacting your organisation, or the **benefits** of the product/service, and in the language your target customers will respond to.

As an alternative to the corporate brochure (or perhaps in conjunction with it) you might consider producing a corporate DVD. Again, you need to consider your target audience, is this something they would be receptive towards? How can your company and its image, its products/services, be communicated via a DVD? Is it the best vehicle for your message? Also consider budgets.

If you produce a catalogue, could you put this on a CD rather than having a printed version? Do you need both? Always consider your target audience and how they would respond to and use a brochure.

Web sites

You might consider making your brochure available as a download through your web site, or perhaps from a page that can be easily printed. Your brochure should reflect the style and design of your web site. Whatever you decide, make sure that your web site reflects your company's image and products, and is designed with your customers in mind. It is not a bit of good having a trendy, flashy web site with tiny print if your customers can't see or access it properly. Remember your customers and make your web site attractive to them.

Make sure that your web site can be easily updated, preferably by you or by a member of your staff. If you need to outsource this, then ensure that the information will be updated quickly and regularly.

Give someone in your team the responsibility for looking after your web site and ensuring that content is kept fresh.

What kind of structure do you need?

One of the most important aspects is keeping the vital information **'above the fold'** which is what your customers immediately see on the screen without having to scroll down. If you are selling products, or have a special offer, then it would be advisable to display it 'above the fold.' Put longer content on interior pages rather than the home page. Once a visitor has clicked to another page they are much more likely to scroll down.

Have a clean and logical hierarchy to your site and good page structure.

Do you need to provide a secure, online buying service? Or would a simple enquiry or 'Contact Us' form suffice for your organisation?

Do you need an online forum where your customers can meet other like-minded customers, or post comments on your services or products?

Content

Write concisely, preferably using no more than twelve words per line. Time is of the essence to most people using the Internet, so users don't want to read reams of text on-line. Research has shown that people tend to scan text on screen. It also harder to read from a computer screen than it is from paper. Here are some further tips:

O   Keep sentences short

O   Frequently highlight important words or phrases

O   Use bullet points or numbered lists where possible and keep page length short

O   Use highlighted links to take your visitor to further information

O   Use plenty of headings, subheadings and white space, which makes it easier to read

O   Avoid centre text and don't use all capitals

O   Avoid excessive italics; use them for emphasis only

O   Check the colours you use aren't bad for those with various forms of colour blindness, if in doubt make it black and white and see if it still makes sense.

O   Always underline links

○ Navigation should be as easy as possible either on the left hand side of the page or across the top. It should take up as little space as possible. Keep it in the same consistent style across the web site

○ Put your logo and other corporate statements in the same place across the web site

○ Use graphics sparingly as they add to the download time. Keep the file as small as possible

○ Test your site on various browser sites and window sizes.

In summary

O   decide if you need a corporate brochure and how you are going to use it

O   what unique selling points or benefits are you going to emphasise in your brochure?

O   don't have too many people involved in the design of a corporate brochure, because they will all have different views about what they like

O   stress the benefits of the customer using or contacting your organisation, or the benefits of the product/service in the language your target customers will respond to

O   an alternative to the corporate brochure could be producing a DVD or CD

O   consider making your brochure available as a download through your web site

O   when designing your web site remember your target audience

O   make your web site quick and easy to use

O   keep important information **'above the fold'**

○ have a clean and logical hierarchy to your site and good page structure

○ write concisely and highlight important words or phrases

○ use highlighted links to take your visitor to further information

○ use plenty of headings, subheadings and white space, which makes it easier to read

○ check the colours you use aren't bad for those with various forms of colour blindness

○ use graphics sparingly as they add to the download time

○ test your site on various browser sites and window sizes.

Chapter 9

Exhibitions

Before agreeing to undertake an exhibition you should ask yourself why you are exhibiting. What do you hope to achieve from it? Here are some objectives for exhibiting:

○ To meet existing customers and improve your relationship with them

○ To meet potential customers, identify new opportunities and prepare the ground for future sales

○ To promote your organisation and its image

○ To inform customers and potential customers of new services/products or changes

○ To obtain sales leads.

Questions to ask before exhibiting

Before exhibiting ask yourself the following:

○ **Is it the right exhibition for my business?**

Are your customers and potential customers going to be there? Who will attend the exhibition?

O **How are the organisers promoting the exhibition?**

Are they going to do enough to attract visitors?

O **What will it cost? You need to consider the following:**

- Cost of the space
- Cost of hiring or producing a stand
- Cost of material
- Cost of your time
- Cost of any lost business whilst you are away.

O **Design of your stand**

Who is responsible for this? What image do you wish to create? The stand should be welcoming and accessible. Corner stands are ideal as access is available from three directions. Alternatively a stand sited at the bottom of a stairwell can prove to be a good location.

Before the exhibition

To maximise the opportunities at the exhibition try and arrange as many appointments as you can with your prospects encouraging them to come and see you on your stand. This gives you a good opportunity to discuss your services/products on neutral territory.

Conduct a campaign to tell them about your presence, send out a mailshot and/or an e-shot, take out some advertising in the relevant trade or consumer publications, or send a press release. Offer an incentive for them if they turn up on your stand. Arrange an on-stand demonstration, if appropriate to your business, and invite them to attend at a certain time.

Literature

Make sure you have the right literature and don't display it too neatly otherwise visitors will be afraid of disturbing your work of art.

It is also a good idea to have something moving on display and I don't mean the staff! A piece of equipment, a computer programme, or a DVD can be ideal. If played loudly it attracts visitors to your stand. But make sure it doesn't run on endlessly. Stop and start it at loud places especially when visitors to your stand are flagging.

Staffing

Make sure you have enough staff manning your stand. You should always have at least two people on the stand for the majority of time. Exhibition work is very tiring and people do need to take a break, have a coffee and go to the toilet. In addition, if you have at least two people, you can have a pre-arranged signal between you to get rid of the time wasters.

After the exhibition

Many organisations fail to track the results of an exhibition. This seems crazy when you think of the amount of money they cost. You must evaluate the success or otherwise of undertaking that exhibition and you must be prepared to track contacts for some time afterwards; months, years even. Look at:

O   How many leads you generated?

O   How many orders you gained?

O   Ask if the exhibition was worth attending and would you do it again

O   How much did it cost you – was this recovered with orders received?

Ruthlessly follow up all contacts made, and keep in touch with them. Use mailshots, e-shots and newsletters to do so.

In summary

O   why are you exhibiting. What do you hope to achieve from it?

O   is it the right exhibition for your business?

O   how are the organisers promoting the exhibition?

O   what will it cost?

O   who is responsible for the design of your stand?

O   have at least two people on the stand for the majority of time

O   track the results of an exhibition

O   ruthlessly follow up all contacts made, and keep in touch with them.

Chapter 10

Sponsorship and sales promotion

Sponsorship

Sponsoring an event or an individual, or working with a charity can be an effective way of communicating your message to your target group of customers, and can give you exposure to new groups of potential customers. It can also position you in the market place. Care though needs to be taken when choosing who or what to sponsor, as you do not wish to run the risk of portraying a negative image.

Decide first what you hope to achieve through sponsorship, i.e. why are you doing it? If it's just the case of buying the local football or cricket team their kit because your son or daughter happens to play for them then that's fine, but that's not really sponsorship in its true sense, it's more of a charitable donation. So, think about your objectives. Here are some to help clarify why you feel sponsorship might be right for your organisation.

Some objectives for sponsorship could be:

❍   To enhance the image or reputation of your organisation

○ To build links in the community

○ To reach a new target audience

○ To promote your company name and image.

How will the target group see your company name and in what connection will it be associated?

How much will you have to pay for the sponsorship and what does this cover? What can you get out of it, for example, additional press coverage, entertaining at an event? Also consider these extra costs.

Are there any other sponsors and if so who are they? Are they your competitors? How long will the sponsorship last?

Maximizing your sponsorship takes time, effort and additional costs over and above what you are paying for the sponsorship; so make sure you have the resources to do it and the commitment to make it work.

It doesn't have to be a big sponsorship deal like the Olympics or the London Marathon; many successful sponsorship deals can be forged between local companies and charities, and other organisations.

Where will the sponsors be advertising, and where can your name be positioned? Will leaflets be given out? What is happening around the event that you could capitalise on, a competition perhaps?

Are you going to organise any corporate hospitality around the event? For example, if you are sponsoring an art exhibition by students of the local art college, you could become one of the judges and you could hold a drinks reception and invite your key customers and prospects to this. An event like this would generate press coverage in the local media and the art media. You could put photographs of winning exhibits on your company web site with a link to the art college and vice versa. Younger people would then be aware of your products and services, particularly relevant if they are your target audience.

Identify your objectives and your target audience and how you can reach them, think creatively and then go out in search of possible sponsorship opportunities.

Sales promotion

Sales promotion as a marketing tool is a short-term activity, rather than a long term one. It is designed to boost sales to a certain product, brand or service.

Sales promotion campaigns have many objectives, they:

○ attract customers to your premises

○ heighten consumer awareness

○ encourage repeat sales

○ increase the penetration of new products

○ boost volume sales.

However, if you have an ailing product or brand, it might be best to consider repackaging and relaunching it, rather than trying to do a promotion to stimulate sales.

Sales promotion activity can also be carried out in conjunction with other parties in the form of sponsorship. For example, collecting tokens from a product packet, (manufacturer) in a certain chain of supermarkets (retailer) to help buy computers for schools (charity/sponsorship). As I mentioned before, you can set up your own local sponsorship and sales promotion opportunities by banding together with local suppliers, retailers, and other organisations.

Charity promotions can have enormous PR impact, and can substantially increase brand awareness, but be careful that you match the correct brand with the correct charity.

Types of sales promotions

This can include:

Tokens

Collecting tokens to be redeemed against a future purchase or to go towards a charity or good cause as previously illustrated with our school example.

Money off coupons

These tend to be very effective in introducing new and improved products. They can reward loyal users and help improve brand loyalty. They can provide an incentive without having to change the price on the packaging.

Competitions

These can be organised fairly quickly and are relatively easy to manage. They also translate well onto a web site. They can secure repeat purchases but unless the value of your prize is high the take up might be slow.

Free samples

This can be expensive and more difficult to administer. If sampling door to door you will need to organise an outside agency to do this for you. Special packs can be expensive.

Other promotions can include:

○ Buy one get one free

○ 25% discount

○ Buy three for two

○ 10% extra

O   Give aways in magazines/newspapers/radio
     campaigns

O   Cut out coupons – children go free, two meals
     for the price of one etc.

O   Personality endorsements

O   Point of sale material

As with all your marketing you must evaluate the success
of it. You need to know from the outset what you wish
to achieve. You might wish to measure the number of
promotional units taken up or sold, number of new
users, or attitudes towards the product from both actual
users and potential users.

Sales promotion should not be viewed in isolation but
should work alongside your other marketing activities.

In summary

O   sponsoring an event, a person, or working with a charity can be an effective way of communicating your message to your target group of customers, and can give you exposure to new groups of potential customers

O   care needs to be taken when choosing who or what to sponsor, as you do not wish to run the risk of portraying a negative image

O   decide first what you hope to achieve through sponsorship

O   how much will you have to pay for the sponsorship and what does this cover?

O   who are the other sponsors, are they your competitors?

O   how long will the sponsorship last?

O   sales promotion is a short-term activity designed to boost sales to a certain product, brand or service

○ types of sales promotions can include:
 - tokens
 - money off coupons
 - competitions
 - free samples
 - buy one get one free
 - 25% discount
 - buy three for two
 - 10% extra
 - give away in magazines and newspapers
 - cut out coupons – children go free, two meals
 for the price of one etc.
 - personality endorsements
 - point of sale material

Chapter 11

Building a media profile

Editorial coverage is an extremely effective way of raising your organisation's profile and stimulating enquiries. It can carry at least two and a half times the weight of advertising.

It can:

O   raise your organisation's visibility and credibility with customers and prospective customers

O   stimulate sales of goods and services

O   set you apart from the competition

O   help to motivate employees – everyone likes to work for a successful organisation

O   help to attract good quality recruits

O   help to reinforce the other sales messages you are sending out.

> The secret to successful media coverage is
> pitching the right story to the right media
> at the right time to convey the right message
> to your target audience

The days when reporters were roving the streets in search of a good news story are long gone, so it is down to you to supply them with the news. You do this by sending in your news stories on a regular basis to the media relevant to your market and your organisation. In this chapter I look at how you can do this but first a few words about the difference between editorial and advertising.

Editorial coverage is not the same as advertising where you have bought the space and can say whatever you like in that space as long as it is decent. Editorial space is 'free' therefore you do not have the same control over what is said. It is up to the media owner, or editor, to decide whether he wishes to use your 'story.'

Your news story **will** get altered and shortened, and the angle might even be changed to one you didn't expect. Journalists do sometimes get names and figures wrong and occasionally misinterpret what you are saying either by accident or, dare I say it, by design but there are ways of writing your news release that will minimise any errors or misinterpretations by the journalist, which I cover later.

You also have no guarantee that your news story will appear. Telephoning the journalist and sounding off is not a good idea. It will only alienate him and guarantee no future coverage. If your story doesn't get used there could be several reasons for this:

O   it has been squeezed out by something else

O   you got the timing wrong and missed the deadline

O   you failed to explain the significance of your mega breakthrough to the journalist

O   your press announcement was boring

O   it was due to plain editorial incompetence!

Perseverance is the key. If your story doesn't get used then move on to the next story and keep a regular steady flow of good news stories going to the journalist. This will help you to build a good relationship with the media.

So what are your possible news stories?

There are many 'news' stories to tell within an organisation. Here are examples of just some of them:

O   winning new orders/contracts

O   retirements

- new appointments

- promotions

- new products or services

- celebrations, like anniversaries

- winning awards

- success of employees

- involvement in local charities

- good financial results

- sales promotions

- sponsorships

- celebrity visits and endorsements

- new literature/free information

- human interest stories – personal achievements

Scan the local and national newspapers to see what makes the news. Look at your trade or professional magazines to see who is hitting the headlines and with what kind of story. Develop a journalistic eye and look for the angle, i.e. the element that makes the story appealing and different. Set yourself targets for writing and distributing at least one press release a month.

A word about angles

You can greatly enhance your news story by strengthening or having an angle. Here are some suggestions.

Urgency

- O New
- O Launched today
- O Re-launched
- O Improved

Uniqueness

- O Believed to be the first
- O Unique product
- O Unique survey
- O The first of its kind

Milestones

- O The one hundredth
- O The first customer
- O The 1,000 customer

Conflict

- O Challenges the report
- O Challenges the Government
- O Warns businesses
- O Warns the public

Special days

O   Valentine's Day
O   Mother's Day
O   November 5th
O   Other anniversaries

Others

O   oldest
O   youngest
O   largest
O   smallest
O   biggest
O   unusual
O   bucking the trend

Where can you send your story?

There are many different types of media. Here are some of them.

O   **National newspapers**
      - Daily newspapers
      - Sunday newspapers

O   **Local newspapers**
      - Daily local newspapers
      - Weekly local newspapers
      -Bi-weekly local newspapers

O **Freesheets**
   - Community newspapers

O **Specialist magazines**
   - Professional and trade press

O **Consumer magazines**

O **Local radio**

O **National radio**

O **Local television**

O **National television including cable and
   satellite channels**

O **Internet sites**

You need to ensure that you send your news story to the most relevant media for your market, so some research will be called for. It is now easy to do this through the Internet by typing into one of the search engines, and then clicking through to the publications, programmes and web sites that you think might be interested in what you have to say. On most of these you will find an e-mail address or an editorial contact or link.

In addition, there are media web sites, community and product web sites that might be eager to receive your news.

Writing the news story

When constructing a 'news release' to tell your news story you need to think in terms of a triangle or pyramid in that the whole story, including the angle, is contained in the first paragraph and then fleshed out in subsequent paragraphs. Here is an example of how to write a news release.

Writing the news release

Headline – an idea of what the story is about

The headline is there to catch the journalist's eye and tell him what the story is about. Your headline will rarely be used by the newspaper or magazine. The journalist, editor or sub editor will put their own title to the story, which best fits the style of their publication. Your headline might only be used if you are writing an article to commission, or if you have paid to see the article printed. In the latter case we are not talking about editorial but advertising or advertorial.

The first paragraph is the key to the release. It must contain the whole story, the angle and your organisation's name, where you are based and what you do.

The second paragraph provides the details already summarised in paragraph one; the facts and figures if necessary. You might only need one paragraph of explanation otherwise two will probably be sufficient.

The third paragraph is the quote and the fourth paragraph might contain more practical facts. If the release is about a new publication or event it can give a contact name and telephone number.

At the end of the news release put ENDS, and the date. Then, 'For further information contact…' and give details of contacts within your company for the journalist or editor.

The diagram below illustrates how the news release is written.

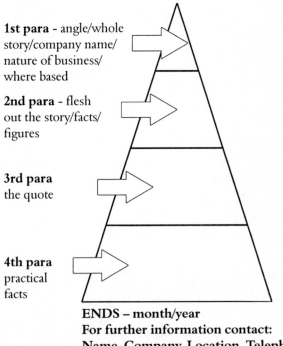

Headline

1st para - angle/whole story/company name/ nature of business/ where based

2nd para - flesh out the story/facts/ figures

3rd para the quote

4th para practical facts

ENDS – month/year
For further information contact:
Name, Company, Location, Telephone
E-mail address and web site.

Writing your news release

○ Write the words 'News Release' at the top of the document, even if you are going to e-mail it to the journalist, radio or television station, or web site. You might also like to put in the subject heading of your e-mail: 'News Release' and your company name, or the headline of your news release.

○ Type your news story neatly with 1.5 spacing and wide margins and use only one side of paper.

○ Don't underline anything and if you go onto a second page put 'more follows....' at the bottom of the first page. Do this even if you are e-mailing the news release as an attachment, but if you are copying it into the e-mail message, then there is obviously no need for this.

○ Don't split a sentence between one page and the next. Staple the pages together and get someone to proof read it for mistakes before it goes out.

○ E-mail it or send it first class post, or fax it. Wherever possible address the journalist by name. Many journalists prefer to receive news releases by e-mail because it is much easier for them to edit the story on line.

Embargoes

Embargoes are normally used when a new product or service is about to be launched, or the information contained in the press release is sensitive and not to be used before a certain date. The media will honour an embargo and it is certainly useful for them from a planning point of view to have information about the story, or product before its official release. The release can then appear in the newspaper or magazine, or on the television or radio, on the day the product is launched.

It is usually common practice to write at the top of your release **'Embargo – Not to be used before midday on (the date).'**

Do not use embargoes unnecessarily as this will only serve to irritate the journalist.

Photo stories

Some news stories will require a photograph. This is called a photo story. So, what makes a good photo story?

The photo stories are those that are primarily **'human interest'** stories. For example:

O   new staff appointments

O   promotions

○   retirements

○   award winners

○   charity events

○   sponsorship.

You can also send photographs with your news releases on:

○   the company moving into new premises

○   a reception with celebrity guest

○   seminars/conferences

○   Mergers/acquisitions/buy outs and buy ins.

To increase your chances of getting your photograph published it needs to be interesting and creative.

> You need to set the scene. Every picture should tell a story

Look at the story your release is telling, does the photograph reflect this?

Using a professional photographer

Wherever possible enlist the services of a professional photographer. This can help you to get your story covered in the media and it will still be cheaper than advertising, and carry more weight.

Some newspapers and magazines will send a press photographer if they think the story warrants it, but this is less frequent these days than it used to be and you can't always rely on this happening. If a press photographer does come to photograph you or your staff then a couple of words of advice:

Do not be bullied or cajoled into shots that you would not like to see in print

---

Don't get into any pose that makes you uncomfortable

When engaging a professional photographer make sure that you brief him thoroughly beforehand, as he may need to bring along additional equipment. Ensure you are available when he arrives. If you keep the photographer waiting can you blame him for charging you for that time!

A professional photographer will try and put people at their ease. Most people hate being photographed. It is an ordeal that many want over and done with as quickly as possible. This means you also need a friendly photographer and one who works quickly. Nobody wants to be standing around forever. This is not a wedding and there is work to be getting on with.

You will need contact sheets of the shots the photographer has taken preferably the same day as the photo shoot or the following one. These can be e-mailed to you and then you can choose the best shots for your news story.

Doing it yourself

If you decide to take the photograph yourself then ensure that you take tight (close-up) shots of people. Also ensure they are high quality digital shots.

Rules for good media relations

○   **Try and understand the media**

Editors and producers have a job to do and that job is to produce newspapers, magazines or programmes that people want to read or listen to. Your task is to provide them with stories that are suitable for their medium.

○   **Always try and be accessible**

The media work to tight deadlines so takes calls or return them quickly. Failure to respond may mean missed coverage for your organisation.

O   **Don't ask to see copy in advance**

Journalists don't like showing you their copy in advance as experience has shown them that some people can't resist dabbling with the style or changing their minds about what they said.

O   **When you are asked for a comment make it a 'sound bite'**

Use conversational English not management speak.

However, if a journalist telephones you for a comment about something you haven't seen, or something that is slightly controversial, you might need time to think about your response. Tell him you will call back within five minutes and then do so. If you do not return the call then you will miss an opportunity for press coverage, and worse the journalist will know that he cannot rely on you so you will lose future coverage.

> Ask the journalist what his deadline is and ensure you call back within that timescale

Be aware of subjects you do not wish to discuss and do not be drawn into discussing them.

Be open and positive and do not lie, as journalists are very good at detecting lies.

Do not make unsupported claims and avoid negative comments.

Do not say anything that you would not wish to see in print.

Do not be aggressive or combative towards a journalist even if they are like that to you.

Stay focused and remain polite.

Ask the journalist what his news slant is, so that you can provide the most useful information.

Always have ready a few well rehearsed statements or key points about your organisation you would like to make. This will help you in leading the interview rather than just responding to it. This is particularly important in television and radio interviewing.

O   **Maintain a friendly relationship with journalists**

If a journalist can rely on you to feed him good stories and provide information then you will increase your chances of winning more media coverage.

O   **Don't hound a journalist to find out when your story is likely to appear**

O   **Don't try and win coverage by overdoing the entertainment**

Journalists know there is no such thing as a free lunch and that you are looking for something in return. You can take them out to lunch to thank them for their co-operation, or to find out if they are interested in any particular news items you might be able to supply. You can also use the meal to explain to them that you are keen to raise your media profile and would like to send them stories that would help them. If you know what they are interested in then hopefully you can supply them with the right stories. Journalists don't mind this at all. Remember they are looking for good stories and you can help save them time and energy by providing these. For more information on this subject including handling a media crisis and television and radio interviews see *The Easy Step by Step Guide to Building a Positive Media Profile.*

In summary

O   media coverage is an extremely effective way of raising your organisation's profile

O   the secret to successful media coverage is in pitching the right story to the right media at the right time

O   there are many 'news' stories to tell within an organisation. Scan the local and national newspapers to see what makes the news

O   look at your trade or professional magazines to see who is hitting the headlines and with what kind of story

O   develop a journalistic eye and look for the angle – the element that makes the story appealing and different

O   keep releases short

O   when constructing a news release you need to think of a triangle or pyramid.

Chapter 12

Word of mouth

Personal recommendation is a powerful marketing tool.

> There is a saying, 'Do good work and more work comes from it'

Loyal and satisfied customers will recommend you and your products and services to others. Therefore, your internal marketing is as important, if not more important, than your external marketing, particularly if you are a service organisation or operating in the public sector. Our sister publication *'Are Your Customers Being Served'* looks at this area in more detail.

In addition, 'word of mouth recommendation' has also taken on a new meaning since the arrival of the Internet.

With the average Briton now spending one hundred and sixty four minutes on the Internet every day, (according to Google) it should come as no surprise that influence through word of mouth in the digital arena is critical to an organisation.

The film and music industry have already harnessed the power of the Internet by tapping into and utilising online opinion formers. Now, when planning a marketing, advertising or promotional campaign, it is simply not enough to think only in terms of the printed and tangible matter but these campaigns need to include and embrace online marketing.

From blogs to social networks the Internet is not just a tool for the young; all ages access and use it. When a campaign takes off it can gather a momentum that can ripple across sales in all channels. The Internet can be buzzing with it.

One such campaign was Hotmail, which by adding the line 'Get your free e-mail at Hotmail' to the end of outgoing e-mails recruited twelve million new subscribers. In 2004, when Google repeated the trick with Gmail, when allowing one thousand opinion formers to 'invite friends' they created three million sign ups within three months.

However the news is spread about your organisation and its products and services, whether that is online or through traditional word of mouth recommendation or campaigns, make sure the message is a positive one.

Having a reputation for good quality products and services can help you to build a solid and growing customer base. You can also enhance this by consistently communicating with your customers and prospective customers through using some of the effective marketing techniques discussed in this book.

For those other techniques that haven't been discussed in this book, like Telemarketing and Selling, which, as I mentioned before, require a high level of personal development skills and special training in sales techniques, you might wish to read our sister publications: *The Easy Step by Step Guide to Telemarketing Cold Calling & Appointment Making*, and *The Easy Step by Step Guide to Successful Selling*.

In summary

To recap then, here are some key marketing messages to help you win more business:

O   take time to identify your target customers and understand what they buy and why they buy

O   be clear about your objectives

O   chose the right marketing tool to communicate in the right way with your target customers

O   understand the language your customers speak and the benefits they are seeking

O   consistently strive to deliver excellence

O   continually search for new ways of delivering what your customers want, and developing new and better services/products.

Business never stands still. If you do nothing then nothing is exactly what you will get in return. Make sure this doesn't happen to you and your organisation.

Good luck!